Guion
THE LION

A Coloring Book

The sun rises on the savannah.

3

"Rae! Wake up!
You have to see this!"
exclaimed Guion the Lion.

Rae the Bushbaby
mumbled,
"I cannot think
of ONE reason
to be excited
right now."

"Ta Da!" Guion squinted his eyes, tilted his head,
and swept his arms out wide.

"I couldn't let my best friend
miss this epic occasion!"

"The kingdom is preparing for battle
against the fierce dragon."

"You woke me up for this?" cried Rae. "An ugly, brown dirt mound and Wilson the Giraffe chewing on leaves?"

9

Guion looked back at the castle
and thought for a minute.

Smiling, he said,
"I know exactly what to
show you, Rae! Let's go!"

Wilson had overheard
her friends and stopped
to take a look.

She squinted her eyes,
tilted her head, and then
she heard the knight say,
"Hello, Giraffe.
Do you seek passage
over our kingdom?"

Determined to share his fun,
Guion guided Rae to the watering hole.

With the help of a long reed and a tilt of his head,
Guion looked at the underwater landscape.

"We've just discovered Queen Anne's Revenge
commanded by Captain Blackbeard."

"Oh, look! We aren't the first-the mermaids
are playing hide-and-seek in the ship."

Eager to see the pirate ship herself,
Rae grabbed the reed. After a moment,
Rae lifted her head and groaned.

"What are you talking about?
There's no ship! It's just Hoke the Hippo
and his buddies taking a soak."

Hoke grabbed a reed and tilted his head,
just like he had seen Guion do.

Hoke smiled widely at the wonders he saw.

Not ready to give up, Guion hollered,
"Keep up, Rae! Let's try one more place!"

As the two friends entered the
savannah, Guion stopped quickly,
squinted, and tilted his head.

"Now, don't be frightened, Rae.
These are friendly dinosaurs."

"What dinosaurs? All I see are some big
trees and Olivia the Ostrich sitting on her nest."

Rae thought about the day.
Why couldn't she see the castle or the mermaids?

Then she remembered that Guion
had squinted his eyes and tilted his head
each time he saw something fantastic.
She could give that a try.

When she saw the terrifying
T. rex, she knew for sure.

Jumping up and down,
she exclaimed, "Holy smokes! I see it!"
And it was the coolest thing she'd ever seen.
Rae couldn't wait to tell Guion.

Rae found her friend sitting alone and asked,
"Hey Guion, what do you see now?"

He turned to her and responded, "A pretty sunset. Right?"
Rae slowly shook her head and said, "No."

"Look at the giant Ferris wheel!" Rae exclaimed.
"And the huge circus tents," said Wilson the Giraffe.
"I can almost taste the cotton candy!" cried Olivia the Ostrich.

Guion looked around at his friends
and a huge smile spread across his face.
"And the fireworks are incredible!" he shouted.